EX LIBRIS

....

The Little Book of

DREAMS

JOAN HANGER

PENGUIN BOOKS

PENGUIN BOOKS

Published by the Penguin Group
Penguin Books Ltd, 80 Strand, London WC2R 0RL, England
Penguin Putnam Inc., 375 Hudson Street, New York, New York 10014, USA
Penguin Books Australia Ltd, Ringwood, Victoria, Australia
Penguin Books Canada Ltd, 10 Alcorn Avenue, Toronto, Ontario, Canada M4V 3B2
Penguin Books (P) Ltd, 11, Community Centre,
Panchsheel Park, New Delhi - 110 017, India
Penguin Books (NZ) Ltd, Cnr Rosedale and Airborne Roads,
Albany, Auckland, New Zealand
Penguin Books (South Africa) (Pty) Ltd, 24 Sturdee Avenue,
Rosebank 2196, South Africa

Penguin Books Ltd, Registered Offices: 80 Strand, London WC2R 0RL, England

www.penguin.com

First published in Australia by Penguin Books Australia Ltd 1998
First published in Great Britain by Penguin Books 1998
19 21 23 25 27 29 30 28 26 24 22 20 18

Copyright © Joan Hanger, 1998
All rights reserved

The moral right of the author has been asserted

Printed in England by William Clowes Ltd
Typeset in Australia by Post Pre-press Group

A NOTE FROM THE AUTHOR

Chances are you have never really given too much serious thought to your dreams. Maybe the occasional bizarre dream led you to share it with someone, but what about the dreams you dream every night? Indeed, can you remember them?

This little book is for those who are interested in dreams and for those who want to understand the special language of dreams.

Understanding your dreams will take some time and patience because dreams are slippery by nature and even the act of recalling your dreams is often difficult. But the rewards are worth the trouble, so be persistent!

Always keep in mind, though, that dream interpretation is not an exact science. In the definitions of dream themes and symbols in this book you will find that there are usually multiple meanings of each. In addition, dream consultants and other books may differ slightly in their interpretation. In the end they can only guide you, for only *you* can discover the real meaning of your dreams.

Learn from your dreams what you lack.

W. H. AUDEN

(1907–73)

SIGMUND FREUD (1865–1939) began the work of understanding dreams in the modern era. He rejected the idea that dreams were a response to events outside of ourselves. Freud believed that at the heart of our dreams lies our deepest, often sexual, desires which our dreams keep hidden from our waking minds.

CARL GUSTAV JUNG (1875–1961) disagreed
with Freud by arguing that dreams were
vital messages designed to be listened
to – not hidden away. Jung was convinced
that dreams help to reveal to our waking
minds many of our deepest wishes,
and by doing so help us to fulfil
our ambitions.

DREAM *n.* **1** a series of pictures or events in the mind of a sleeping person. **2** a daydream or fantasy. **3** an ideal, aspiration, or ambition, esp. of a nation. **4** a beautiful or ideal person or thing.

THE CONCISE OXFORD DICTIONARY

Remember: everything and everyone in your dream is a PART OF YOU, from the shadow in the corner to the flowers in the background to the paper on which a letter was written. Take the time to discover what each symbol means and you'll discover a lot about yourself.

RAPID EYE MOVEMENT (REM) sleep is a
phase of shallow sleep that occurs several
times during a night. It is so called
because our eyes flicker rapidly during
this time . . .

Ironically we dream most vividly during REM phases of sleep yet our muscles are paralysed at these times. This may explain why we often dream of being UNABLE TO RUN AWAY from a frightening pursuer.

The poet and the dreamer are distinct,
Diverse, sheer opposite, antipodes.
The one pours out a balm upon the
    world,
The other vexes it.

JOHN KEATS
(1795–1821)

Some dream theories suggest that not everyone dreams in COLOUR and that only those who are particularly colour-perceptive in their waking lives are likely to do so. The next time you dream, try to remember whether your dream was in colour. Note any striking colours and analyse them separately, as they will be giving you a new message.

To help you remember and understand your dreams, keep a DREAM DIARY beside your bed. As soon as you wake up, write down *everything* you remember about your dream, especially your feelings . . .

To help you begin your dream diary, try this simple 5-STEP PROCESS:

1 Record your dream.
2 Examine your dream.
3 Note your feelings.
4 Note previous day's events.
5 Summarise what you think your dream is about.

When WEIGHT GAIN or SWELLING occurs
in dreams, it is often pointing to our
need for praise and flattery. The excess
weight symbolises the ways in which we
may be draining life from others.

Dreams help us to resolve problems,
face fears and indulge passions. Therefore
it is no coincidence that your dreams
almost always feature people, places and
situations about which you have
STRONG FEELINGS.

There is some ill a-brewing towards
 my rest,
For I did dream of money-bags to-night.

WILLIAM SHAKESPEARE

(1564–1616)

If the colour WHITE features prominently
in your dream, you are likely to be
experiencing a feeling of hope and
positiveness in your waking life. The
events in the dream and your feelings
about it will tell you a lot more about the
nature of your optimism.

Did you know that ALCOHOL has a
dampening effect on your sleeping mind
and that it actually discourages dreaming?

THE SHADOW is a frightening figure or presence in dreams. It can 'chase' us, remain as an uncomfortable presence or enter the dream unexpectedly. The Shadow represents the darker side of our personalities, and offers us the opportunity to confront painful aspects of ourselves.

Dreams of being BALD are anxiety dreams for both men and women. The anxiety lies not only in the threat of losing hair, but also in the idea that the baldness reflects a lack of intellect or creativity.

Fɪsʜ have a strong spiritual significance
in dreams. They represent an emerging
life force, and can indicate that a new
you – spiritual or sexual – is about to
spring forth.

The RIGHT SIDE OF THE BRAIN is
responsible for creativity and imagery,
while the left side is concerned with
rational and analytical thinking. You may
expect, therefore, that dreaming takes
place in the right side, but this is not
true. The left side can also dream,
although these dreams are less symbolic
and less imaginative.

Dreams of committing ADULTERY can
express a desire for that person or simply
guilt at having even considered such a
liaison! Adultery dreams may also
suggest a release of sexual feelings.

Dreams of WATER are often connected to the dreamer's emotions. For example, dreams of floating calmly in warm water suggest a waking life of general contentment. Dreams of being caught in rough seas where the dreamer fears drowning almost certainly suggest some insecurity!

Dreams, books, are each a world; and
  books, we know,
Are a substantial world, both pure and
  good.
Round these, with tendrils strong as flesh
  and blood,
Our pastime and our happiness will
  grow.

WILLIAM WORDSWORTH
(1770–1850)

The first step to UNDERSTANDING YOUR DREAMS is accepting that they are not logical extensions of your daily life. Dreams are the product of your sleep. They cannot be understood in the same way that emotions and events in your waking life are.

REUNIONS in dreams recall a sense of nostalgia. Maybe a person or incident from your past has something to offer your life now. On the other hand, your dream could be pushing you to move beyond the past and into the future.

In ancient times, dreams were thought to
be either some kind of SUPERNATURAL
COMMUNICATION or DIVINE MESSAGES from
the gods.

Dreams of TESTS or EXAMS could indicate
that you are undergoing a 'test' of some
kind in your waking life. It may be that
you feel you must stretch your abilities
to the limit in your professional life or
even in your personal life. You may
be experiencing self-doubt or a fear
of failure.

Did you know that BABIES also appear to dream? Babies spend a good deal of their sleeping time in REM (or dreaming) sleep, although unfortunately we cannot know what it is they are dreaming about!

I am melancholy when thou art absent;
look like an ass when thou art present;
wake for thee, when I should sleep,
and even dream of thee, when I am
awake . . . If this be not love, it is
madness, and then it is pardonable . . .

WILLIAM CONGREVE

(1670–1729)

Dreams of being ATTACKED or being
threatened with attack may be a warning
that you are under attack – not
necessarily physically, but perhaps
morally and emotionally – in real life.

Dreams are MESSAGES from yourself to
yourself. Only *you* can interpret the
special meaning in your dreams.

If you dream of being dressed in TOO
MANY CLOTHES or are unable to remove
your clothes, perhaps you are being too
cautious in the relationships in your
waking life. You may have a strong desire
to protect yourself.

While dreams are highly personal, some dreams are expressed in the same pattern by people across all cultures, religions and social classes. These collective dreams are known as ARCHETYPES.

HOUSES represent the physical self and therefore often feature in health-related dreams. For example, a house on fire can suggest the dreamer is experiencing ulcers or indigestion. Pay attention to the state of the house and its surrounds. It can tell you much about your physical and mental health.

Why try to understand your dreams,
you ask? Like your love life, your
working life or your sex life, your dream
life is ANOTHER DIMENSION of yourself – a
dimension available only to you. Can
you bear to leave it unexplored?

CLIMBING dreams symbolise our climb towards our ambitions. Note how far up the ladder you've climbed. Are you exhausted by the climb? Can you keep going? Are you afraid of falling?

Day and night, aloof, from the high
    towers
And terraces, the Earth and Ocean seem
To sleep in one another's arms, and
    dream
Of waves, flowers, clouds, woods, rocks,
    and all that we
Read in their smiles, and call reality.

MARY WOLLSTONECRAFT SHELLEY

(1797–1851)

It may surprise you to know that despite
many theories about WHY WE DREAM or
even why we sleep, no-one has actually
discovered a scientific reason for either
phenomenon.

Simply *wanting* to recall your dreams can actually help you to do so. The act of telling yourself before you go to sleep that you will remember your dreams can help to IMPROVE YOUR RECALL dramatically.

We dream in an anniversary fashion; that is, we dream similar dreams at similar times in our lives. But it is only by keeping a dream diary that we can become aware of our DREAM 'ANNIVERSARIES'.

Despite their name, DAYDREAMS are not exactly dreams. They actually have more to do with fulfilling your wishes and perhaps even with meditation. Daydreams can also express your undeveloped potential.

Having a dream in which you are
WALKING WITHOUT SHOES can indicate
that you are currently going through
a difficult time. Alternatively it can
symbolise a freedom from everyday
responsibilities.

There are many tales of dreams that have forewarned the dreamer of an impending ACCIDENT. If you dream of an accident involving a piece of equipment you use regularly, have it checked. It could well be that your unconscious has noticed some deterioration that could cause an accident.

If you are a woman dreaming you are a MAN, you are generally trying to integrate elements of traditional masculinity (rationality, courage) into your life.

If you are a man dreaming you are a
WOMAN, you are generally being
confronted with the traditional feminine
aspects (intuition, sensitivity) of your
personality that need to be expressed.

It is not surprising that our dreams often involve our experiencing feelings of GUILT. Dreams bring to the forefront our behaviour and feelings – towards others and ourselves – that we may try to repress in our waking lives.

If you find yourself dreaming of BOXING, WRESTLING or KARATE when you have nothing to do with these sports in your waking life you may actually be playing out a real-life contest between a real-life opponent. You may also be wrestling with a problem.

The inability to remember any of your dreams is called DREAM AMNESIA. Sigmund Freud believed that this was our mind's way of protecting itself from disturbing images and desires.

Dreaming of an ISLAND or islands can symbolise one of two things: a distinct sense of isolation or a need for peace and tranquillity.

Analysing your dreams achieves nothing if it remains a purely intellectual exercise. You have to FEEL YOUR DREAMS; you have to want to incorporate their messages into your everyday life for dream analysis to be meaningful.

Some common DREAM THEMES include:
houses
spiders
being naked
losing teeth

It is very rare for a dreamer to hear MUSIC in a dream, so when it occurs it will be delivering a strong message. Music symbolises creative talents. If the music is harmonious, creative talents are being utilised effectively; if not, then perhaps creative talents are being distorted in some way.

There's a long, long trail a-winding
Into the land of my dreams,
Where the nightingales are singing
And a white moon beams:
There's a long, long night of waiting
Until my dreams all come true;
Till the day when I'll be going down
That long, long trail with you.

STODDARD KING

(1889–1933)

It is in our dreams that we fly, enjoy magical people and places, and experience strange encounters and adventures. It is in our dreams that the past, the present and the future merge into one and yet seem to disappear at the same time. No wonder WE CANNOT HELP BUT BE MOVED BY OUR DREAMS!

Dreams of SCISSORS and precise cutting
indicate control and decisiveness in the
waking life of the dreamer.

RECURRING DREAMS can often mean that
the message of the dream has not been
properly understood or confronted by
the dreamer. This is why it continues to
repeat itself. Recurring dreams can also
refer to a traumatic event that has been
left unresolved.

Dreams are elusive – just as you think
you have remembered them, the details
slip away. Therefore, PAPER AND A PEN are
the most important tools you need to
begin working with your dreams.

The word 'NIGHTMARE' actually means 'night demon'. Nightmares express your real-life demons, your deeply held fears and anxieties. Paying attention to your nightmares can help you to identify your fears.

Sigmund Freud – the 'father' of dream analysis in the modern era – once said that his FAVOURITE DREAM was being naked in a crowd of strangers!

Dreams about CROSS-DRESSING may well reflect a hidden waking desire to do so, but it is more likely to be a reflection of some discomfort you feel in the roles your gender forces you to play as either a man or a woman.

DREAMS have been described as
'continuances of the day' and 'rushes
from the heart'.

For each age is a dream that is dying,
  Or one that is coming to birth.
  ARTHUR WILLIAM EDGAR O'SHAUGHNESSY

(1844–81)

Beware of interpreting your dreams too
literally. Falling off a cliff in your dream
does not necessarily mean you'll do so in
real life! This dream could be simply
pointing to a feeling of powerlessness.
Learn to understand the SYMBOLIC NATURE
of your dreams.

Many people have dreams that involve the shedding of BLOOD. While such dreams can be disturbing, they are actually positive. Blood in dreams symbolises completion and sacrifice; the ordeal is over, the healing can begin.

Because we experience the longest phase of REM (or dreaming) sleep just BEFORE WE WAKE UP, it makes sense that we are more likely to remember these dreams before any others.

Dreams of being NAKED have nothing to
do with sex. Such dreams suggest
emotional exposure or vulnerability.
Perhaps you feel you are pretending to
be someone you are not, or maybe you
feel your weaknesses have been exposed.

Studies of sleeping ANIMALS have
suggested that animals also dream.
Mammals have been observed growling,
and moving their paws as though
running, in their sleep.

Did you know that the study of dreams
is called ONEIROLOGY?

Fanatics have their dreams, wherewith
 they weave
A paradise for a sect.

JOHN KEATS

(1795–1821)

SLEEPWALKING actually doesn't have anything to do with dreaming. It occurs outside of REM (or dreaming) sleep when the body is mobile. The best way to deal with sleepwalkers is to lead them back to bed. You shouldn't leave them to continue on their way as they can hurt themselves, but there is no need to wake them up.

The mouth is a symbol of self-image –
both visually and verbally. Dreams of
LOSING TEETH, therefore, suggest that
someone or something is diminishing
your self-image. It may also suggest that
you are feeling inhibited in some way.

While some people say they cannot remember their dreams, WE ALL DREAM at least four or five times every night.

Dreaming of a house ALARM going off refers to your family. Perhaps a member of your family is in need of your help or protection at this time.

You are most likely feeling happy and optimistic if your dreams feature the colours YELLOW and ORANGE. These hopeful dreams could be encouraging you to work towards your goals.

It has been said there is a mythical bird called the PHOENIX inside all of us. The Phoenix enables us to live every moment of our lives to the full, and helps us to overcome each and every challenge.

BOATS are a symbol of our life's journey
and the way in which we negotiate
'rough' and 'smooth' conditions. A classic
boat dream is that of travelling alone in a
boat at night. This symbolises a journey
into the unconscious and a searching for
one's connection to life.

Dreams are almost always associated
with episodes, thoughts and feelings of
THE PREVIOUS DAY. And while you may
think they are trivial, remember your
dreaming mind dramatises seemingly
unimportant details to bring them to
your attention.

I slept, and dreamed that life was Beauty;
I woke, and found that life was Duty.

ELLEN STURGIS HOOPER

(1816–41)

Dreams of WIND can symbolise unsettled emotions or even a need for change in your life.

Dreaming of BABIES or of having a baby usually symbolises a surge of creativity in your waking life. Perhaps you are about to begin a new job or personal project. The need to nurture and protect things that are fragile is another reason why this dream may occur.

Dreams appear to compensate for GAPS and IMBALANCES that exist in our waking lives. This sometimes makes our dreams difficult to understand and can make them difficult to accept. The key to overcoming these imbalances is, of course, conducting an honest analysis of our own dreams.

We are all NATURAL DREAMERS.

REM (or dreaming) sleep is vital to maintaining our overall health. Research has shown that DEPRIVING PEOPLE OF REM SLEEP can lead to hand tremors, memory loss, hallucinations and, more seriously, psychotic or paranoid behaviour.

Have you ever had a particularly vivid dream of a relative or close friend? Maybe the person was dead and reappeared? These dreams are called VISITATION DREAMS and reflect a strong emotional bond with the person.

To die: to sleep;
To sleep: perchance to dream: ay, there's
   the rub;
For in that sleep of death what dreams
   may come . . .

WILLIAM SHAKESPEARE

(1564–1616)

Consider leaving space in your dream diary for DRAWINGS. Perhaps write on one side of the page only, leaving the reverse free for rough sketches of your dream people or landscapes. These sketches can be particularly useful in bringing your dreams to life.

Dreams can often warn us of forthcoming HEALTH PROBLEMS. These often persistent dreams feature powerful symbols and leave the dreamer with a strong physical sense of foreboding upon awakening.

Dreaming of PEOPLE YOU KNOW is your
mind's way of making you aware of
qualities and feelings that you desire.
The qualities and feelings expressed in
your dream interaction with the person
you know will be those you are
becoming aware of in real life . . .

Dreaming of PEOPLE YOU DON'T KNOW is a way of confronting hidden aspects of yourself. Ask yourself what this person in your dream means to you. Do you like this person? What, then, does this say about these hidden aspects of yourself?

The importance of dreams was recognised centuries ago. In Egypt in 2000 BC, DREAM TEMPLES were built especially for priests to interpret the dreams of others.

Real PHYSICAL SENSATIONS experienced by
your body as you dream can influence
the content of your dreams. For
example, a cold wind blowing through
your window can transform itself into
dreams of sailing and storms.

As RED is the colour of passion, heat, fire and anger, dreams that feature the colour red can symbolise any one of these things. It could also point to your energy levels: are you directing your energies in the most efficient way?

Finding KEYS in your dream represents
confidence and domestic bliss, while
dreaming of broken keys symbolises
jealousy or separation. Unlocking a door
with a key points to the existence of new
friends or even lovers!

If the life that you dream is the life that
you have, what more could you want?

TERRY HOLMES

In any study of dreams you will come across the word PSYCHE. The psyche is a part of your consciousness. It is your spiritual, intuitive self – your soul. Your dreams provide an avenue through which your psyche can speak to you.

Dreams of PEARLS represent pleasure and
purity, particularly if you find yourself
admiring them. Discovering pearls in
an oyster symbolises an uncovering
of secrets.

While it is often suggested that MEN'S DREAMS are overwhelmingly sexual, studies have not shown this to be the case!

In Australian Aboriginal culture, DREAMINGS are Ancestral Beings that individual Aborigines or groups claim as their spiritual identity (or totem). Despite their name, the Dreamings are not the products of everyday dreams . . .

The spiritual world in which these Dreamings exist is called THE DREAMING or the Dreamtime. This is often known as the beginning of the world in Aboriginal mythology because it is here that the Dreamings created the world and the patterns and cycles of life. Everyday dreams offer a way of getting in touch with the Dreaming.

Dreams of FLYING are common and are very positive. Flying symbolises ambition, achievement and freedom, and dreams of flying are often enjoyed by successful people who have a high profile. Flying dreams are associated with feelings of great happiness and power.

Did you know that fever, withdrawal
from medication, lack of sleep,
indigestion and allergies can all
CAUSE NIGHTMARES?

DRIVING A CAR in your dreams symbolises
the way in which you 'drive' through
life. Pay attention to your driving dreams.
Are you the driver or the passenger? Are
you in reverse or unable to start your car?
Is your foot on the brake but the car
won't stop?

The FEELINGS you have upon awakening from a dream are the key to your understanding of the dream. You may have dreamt of being chased but woke up laughing. This dream will mean something quite different from the same dream after which you have awoken in fear.

More common DREAM THEMES . . .
falling
being chased
being late
being paralysed

And one day there will come a great
awakening when we shall realise that life
itself was a great dream.

CHUANG-TZU

(c. 350 BC)

Recurring dreams are rarely identical even though you may think they are. There are usually DIFFERENCES – however small – and the meaning of the dreams is often contained in these differences.

Studies have shown that anxious people dream ANXIOUS DREAMS more often than others. Similarly, depressed people dream DEPRESSING DREAMS more often than others. However, medication could heighten such dreams.

Have you ever been aware you were dreaming and actually controlled the direction of your dream? This conscious dreaming is called LUCID DREAMING, and it occurs to only a small number of people.

The common advice 'sleep on it' suggests something of the PROBLEM-SOLVING nature of dreams. Indeed, throughout history many great scientific and technological inventions came about as the result of dreams.

It can be a frightening experience to look into a MIRROR in your dream and have a strange face stare back at you. This situation represents an identity crisis of some sort. Look carefully at the face in the mirror. Is the face familiar? How do you feel about the reflection?

Dreams and the light imaginings of men,
And all that faith creates or love desires,
Terrible, strange, sublime and beauteous
   shapes.

MARY WOLLSTONECRAFT SHELLEY
(1797–1851)

Why keep a dream diary? A dream diary
will help you to recognise recurring
themes and images in your dreams, and
will let you chart their progress over time.
It is the best way of RECORDING, ANALYSING
and UNDERSTANDING your dreams.

Some psychologists believe that continually dreaming of PARALYSIS is a signal that your diet needs changing. If you find yourself dreaming of paralysis regularly, perhaps you should look closely at your diet.

When a MAN DREAMS OF BABIES he is
usually questioning the feminine aspect
of his being. Such dreams are also
strongly associated with the birth of
creativity in waking life. On a more
literal level, men with pregnant partners
are likely to have dreams that they, too,
are pregnant.

The next time you dream, try to
remember if you were ACTIVE in your
dream or if you were a PASSIVE observer.
Chances are that whatever you are in
your dreams reflects what you are in
your waking life.

Earlier this century, J. W. DUNNE dreamed
he was on an island on which a volcano
was about to erupt. In his dream he tried
to warn the French authorities about the
impending explosion and that 4000 lives
were in danger . . .

A few days later, DUNNE read of the
eruption of Mont Pelee on the French
island of Martinique where it was
estimated that 40 000 lives had
been lost!

Snow symbolises purification and transformation. It can also refer to icy emotions. If your dreams involve snow, you may need to look closely at your emotions. Are you 'cold' and lacking warmth?

And sometimes, when we are awake
and still under the full impact of [our
dream], we cannot but feel that never
in our life has the real world offered us
its equal.

F. W. HILDEBRANDT

The SETTING of your dream is crucial. It provides clues to the central issue of your dream and is vital to your understanding of it.

Some people say that sleeping on your back can cause nightmares, but there is absolutely no truth to this claim. In fact, we change SLEEPING POSITIONS at least eight times during the most peaceful of sleeps.

Dreams about a person who has died
usually symbolise our attempts to deal
with our feelings associated with that
person or indeed with DEATH itself.

OSCAR WILDE, Irish playwright of the
nineteenth century, insisted he could
never travel without his dream diary.

In ancient times the sick were brought to sacred sites, their bodies prepared with bandages and herbs. It was thought that in their sleep they would be visited by the HEALER-GOD ASKLEPIOS, whose spirit would enter the souls of the dreamers and heal their sickness.

Some people have been known to dream the names of RACE WINNERS. While this is not terribly common, some such dreamers claim to have various strategies that could help others to do the same!

What if you slept,
and what if in your sleep you dreamed,
and what if in your dream you went to
　　heaven,
and there you plucked a strange and
　　beautiful flower,
and what if when you awoke you had
　　the flower in your hand?
Oh, what then.

SAMUEL TAYLOR COLERIDGE
(1772–1834)

Have you ever dreamt that you MISSED
YOUR BUS or misplaced your keys or were
unable to make an emergency telephone
call? Such dreams suggest frustration and
anxiety in your waking life, and are
reminders of the stresses under which
you may be putting your body.

Dreams that feature a general blackness or BLACK objects are usually reflecting a feeling of depression in the waking life of the dreamer. Being a negative colour, black can also symbolise our unknown or hidden side.

If reaching out for a pen and paper on which to record your dreams seems too cumbersome, try recording your dreams directly onto a TAPE RECORDER. However as the benefits of recording your dreams are in reading them and looking for patterns, you'll need to write them down eventually.

FOOD dreams symbolise nourishment
and can point to greedy behaviour or
feelings of neglect in your waking life.
It is also often connected with sexuality
and sensuality. If you dream of food,
take note of your feelings in your dream.
Do you feel guilty as you eat? Are you
ravenous and eat to excess?

Every human relationship takes time and requires a degree of effort. In the same way you need time, patience and persistence to cultivate a RELATIONSHIP WITH YOUR DREAMS. And, as with all worthwhile relationships, the rewards are plenty!

As in real life, a RAINBOW in your dreams symbolises hope, healing and new beginnings.

During our four or five cycles of REM (or dreaming) sleep each night, we experience between sixty to ninety minutes of DREAM TIME. Some dreams also occur outside of REM phases of sleep.

Some people use their LUCKY DREAM
NUMBERS for the races or lotto. To work
out your dream number, think about
your dream and identify the key theme
or themes. For example, your theme
could be 'Naked'. Using the table
opposite, your dream number would be
13 (N=1 A=5 K=4 E=1 D=2).

THE DREAM NUMBER TABLE

5	4	3	2	1	9	8	7	6
A	B	C	D	E	F	G	H	I
J	K	L	M	N	O	P	Q	R
S	T	U	V	W	X	Y	Z	

And he dreamed, and behold a ladder
set up on the earth, and the top of it
reached to heaven: and behold the angels
of God ascending and descending on it.

GENESIS 28:12

SPIDERS in dreams can signify a range of possible meanings. A dream of a spider spinning a web is a positive dream symbolising your ability to be part of this creative world. Dreams of many spiders can point to an overwhelming number of responsibilities that you need to address.

Dream interpretation is not infallible.
View the lessons learned in your dream
as you would the ADVICE of a friend:
sometimes it is good, sometimes it
is useful but not too practical, and
sometimes it is seemingly way off
the mark!

The presence of unusually strong and
vivid colours in a dream often signifies a
TURNING POINT in one's life.

Men and women often report having erotic dreams involving CELEBRITIES and FILM STARS. Such dreams often simply indicate a need for excitement and are harmless, so enjoy them!

Dreaming of your own INTESTINES may
suggest that you are about to receive
some grave news from a person close to
you. It could also suggest that a serious
situation is looming. It is a good idea
to see your doctor if this dream
occurs often.

It appears that dreams are often more vivid during PREGNANCY as a result of hormonal changes. The period of REM (or dreaming) sleep is reportedly longer during this time, resulting in dreams that are more complex and often sexier than usual.

A BRIDGE in a dream symbolises a crossing
from one phase of life to another, or
perhaps even a change of emphasis.
It signifies change and progression.

The presence of the colour GREEN in your dreams may point to your awareness of environmental issues and your attitude towards them. It could also reflect a degree of jealousy towards another person.

NIGHT TERRORS are experienced by
children. The dreamer wakes up in
extreme fright but there is no memory
of what has caused it. While hereditary,
environmental and emotional factors
may all play their part, the actual cause
of night terrors remains the subject of
further research.

Some people can predict events, outcomes and encounters in their dreams – whether good or bad, big or small. These dreams are called PREMONITION DREAMS, but they are often called visions, prophecies or even extrasensory perception (ESP).

Dreaming of GUNS can suggest a number
of things. Perhaps you find yourself
constantly disagreeing with those around
you. If the gun is pointed at you, this
could suggest guilt and a desire to
punish yourself. A gun that fails to
fire symbolises powerlessness or
even impotence.

It was a dream of perfect bliss,
Too beautiful to last.

THOMAS HAYNES BAYLY

(1797–1839)

Dreaming of the TELEPHONE is a common dream theme that can reflect the state of your communication with those you care for most. Do you find that you can't get through on the phone? Perhaps you need to have more persistence when it comes to speaking your mind.

Everyone has different dream symbols that indicate their levels of STRESS. Common dream themes related to stress include dreams of death, houses, missing the bus, and going to work only partly clothed. What dream symbol is *your* body's stress symbol?

It is often thought that if you dream of seeing yourself HIT THE GROUND after a big fall you would die in your sleep. The truth is that most dreamers don't report distress on landing and that the ground often becomes soft and inviting.

Dreams don't offer a means of escape from REALITY; they offer the opportunity to enrich and enhance our reality.

About the Author

Joan Hanger is an expert throughout Australasia
on dream analysis, yet she originally learned about
dreams by discussing them with her children over
the kitchen table! She then went on to study at
the C. G. Jung Institute in Zurich, Switzerland,
and now talks dreams with the world through
regular national television appearances in
Australia, and via BBC in London and CNN
in the United States. Joan is also the author of
In Your Dreams and *Wake Up to Your Dreams*.

To all, to each, a fair good-night,
And pleasing dreams, and slumbers
   light!

SIR WALTER SCOTT

(1771–1832)